Women Who Rock

BETHANY Mota

GAIL TERP

BLACK
RABBIT
BOOKS

Bolt is published by Black Rabbit Books
P.O. Box 3263, Mankato, Minnesota, 56002.
www.blackrabbitbooks.com
Copyright © 2017 Black Rabbit Books

Design and Production by Michael Sellner
Photo Research by Rhonda Milbrett

Library of Congress Control Number: 2015954916

HC ISBN: 978-1-68072-068-6   PB ISBN: 978-1-68072-318-2

Printed in the United States at CG Book Printers,
North Mankato, Minnesota, 56003. PO #1799 4/16

Image Credits
Alamy: Everett Collection Inc.,
Cover; AP Images: Courtesy of Bethany Mota, 24; Facebook.com: Bethany
Mota, 8 (right), 9 (top); Getty: Anna Webber,
23 (bottom), Bob Chamberlin, 7, Craig Barritt,
16, 23 (top), FilmMagic, 12, 17, Jon Kopaloff, 8–9
(left), Laura Cavanaugh, 4–5, 14–15 (background),
15, Paul Zimmerman, 27, Timothy Hiatt, 9 (bottom),
21 (top); Newscom: FS2 WENN Photos, 20, Patrick
McMullan.co/McMullan/Sipa USA, 21 (bottom),
28–29 (background); The White House/Sipa USA, 24;
Shutterstock: FashionStock.com, Back Cover, 3, 14,
Helga Esteb, 22, Jaguar PS, 11, Jeff Metzger, 3, 31,
tobuart, 13, 25
Every effort has been made to contact copyright holders for material reproduced
in this book. Any omissions will be
rectified in subsequent printings
if notice is given to the
publisher.

Contents

CHAPTER 1

Overcoming Bullying

It had been a tough year for Bethany Mota. People had been **cyberbullying** her. She felt so sad. She stayed in bed most days. Nothing made her happy.

But then Mota started watching makeup videos on YouTube. The videos **inspired** her to make her own. Her first video showed the makeup she'd bought. It was the start of something big.

Huge Success

Mota **uploaded** her first video in 2009. She was 13 years old. She made more videos. Soon, she had 100 subscribers. By 2015, she had millions of followers. Mota is a **role model** for her fans. She inspires them to be who they want to be. And it all started with one video.

Mota's YouTube Success

220,000

645,000

July 2011

July 2012

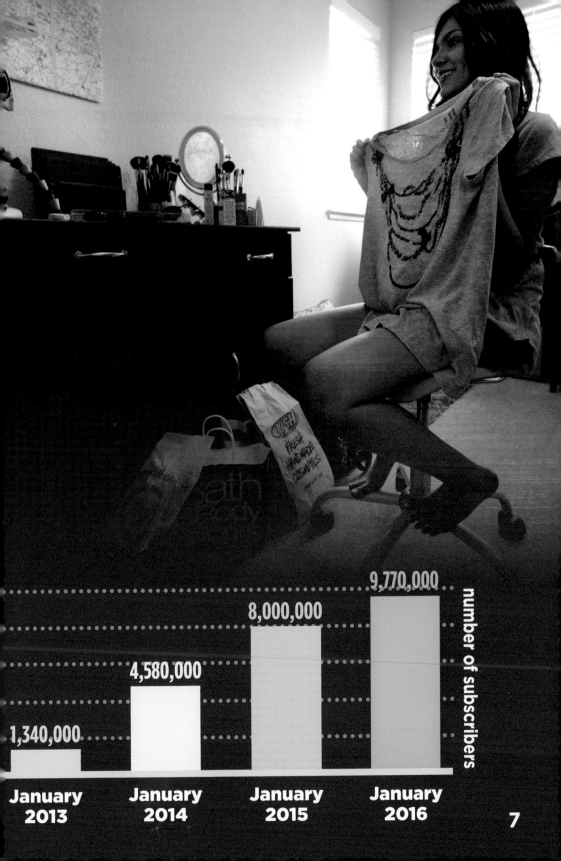

9,770,000

8,000,000

number of subscribers

4,580,000

1,340,000

January 2013	January 2014	January 2015	January 2016

7

Fun Facts

HAS A DOG
NAMED
WINNIE

LOVES TO TRAVEL

LOVES
OWLS

6'

5'

4'

WAS A VERY SHY CHILD

HER NICKNAME IS BETHERS.

HER FANS ARE CALLED MOTAVATORS.

5 feet 4 inches (1.6 m) tall

3'   2'   1'   0

CHAPTER 2

Early Years

Mota was born November 7, 1995. Until third grade, her parents **homeschooled** her. Going to public school was scary at first. In time, Mota made friends.

But in eighth grade, shy Mota asked to be homeschooled again. She felt school was too stressful.

> For fun, Mota took dance lessons. She made friends in that activity.

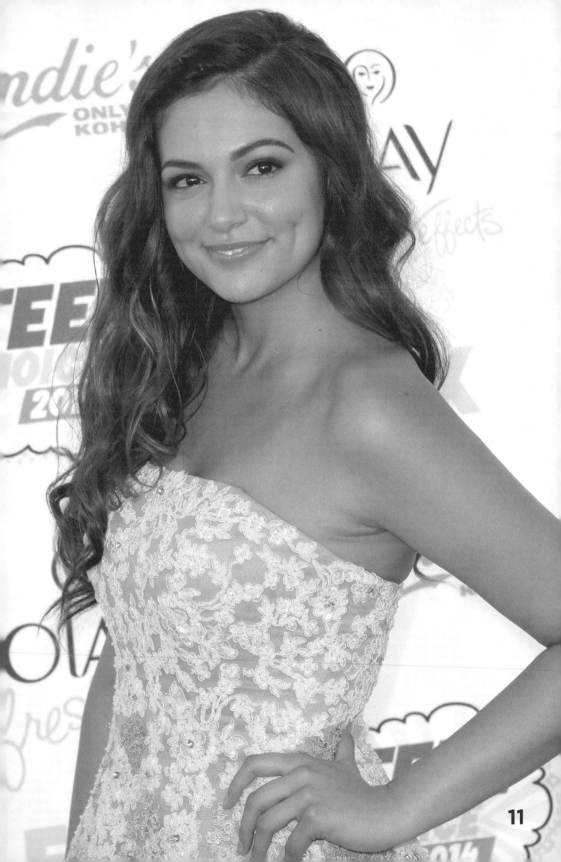

Dealing with Hard Times

Things were going well for Mota. But then the cyberbullying started. A girl she knew posted mean things about Mota online. Her two best friends stopped being her friends.

The bullying really hurt, and Mota didn't know what to do. Then she discovered the videos. Making videos helped Mota deal with her sadness. Talking to a camera came easily to her. She started sharing about things she loves.

1 HAUL VIDEOS
MAKEUP CLOTHES JEWELRY

MOTA'S 2 ROUTINES
GETTING UP IN THE MORNING
GETTING READY FOR BED

ADVICE 3
HAVING CONFIDENCE
KNOWING YOUR INNER BEAUTY
DEALING WITH BULLYING

4 BEDROOM MAKEOVERS

DECORATING
ORGANIZING
CLEANING

5
BACK TO SCHOOL

LOCKER ORGANIZATION
HAIR, MAKEUP, AND OUTFITS
EASY BREAKFASTS

6 DIY PROJECTS

SNACKS
JEWELRY
CLOTHES

CHAPTER 3

Making It Big

A lot happened after that first video. Mota made more videos. More people watched them. Businesses placed ads on her YouTube page. These ads earned her money. The money added up. Soon Mota was worth more than $3 million. And she was still in her teens!

MUSIC RECORDING
She recorded "Need You Right Now"
and made a music video

MOTA'S FOLLOWERS
AS OF
NOVEMBER 2015

YouTube	
Facebook	1,700,000
Instagram	
Twitter	2,700,000

Social Networking Queen

Mota also joined Twitter and Facebook. In 2011, she joined Instagram. Mota connects with her fans on these sites. She tells them she loves them. She encourages them to stand up for themselves. As a result, Mota has millions of fans.

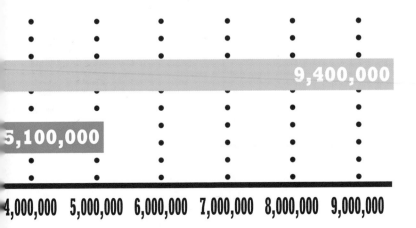

Beyond the Videos

When she's not making videos, Mota is still busy. She's singing, dancing, and acting.

MOTA WAS THE FIRST YOUTUBER ON THE SHOW. SHE GOT 4TH PLACE.

Mota
Mania

FASHION DESIGNING

SHE CREATES CLOTHING, JEWELRY, AND BEDDING DESIGNS FOR AÉROPOSTALE.

MOTA HAS APPEARED ON MORE THAN 20 TV SHOWS.

DANCING WITH THE STARS

CHAPTER 4

Mota Today

Mota travels to see her fans. She goes all over the United States to meet them. Her tour bus takes her from place to place. She always has long lines of fans. Mota meets with fans outside the United States too. She's been to Asia, Canada, and Australia.

Interview with Obama

In 2015, Mota **interviewed** President Obama. She was one of three YouTube stars to have the honor. They met Obama at the White House. Mota asked him about bullying. Obama said that she could fight bullying better than he could. He said she shows others how to speak up against what's wrong.

Mota helped UNICEF raise money for schools. People who donated earned a chance to have lunch with Mota.

Using Her Fame

In all she does, Mota reaches out to fans. She wants them to love who they are. She spreads that message in her videos. Mota is a role model. She uses her fame to help others.

In 2014, Mota earned the Streamy Award for Fashion. She also won the 2014 and 2015 Teen Choice Web Star Award.

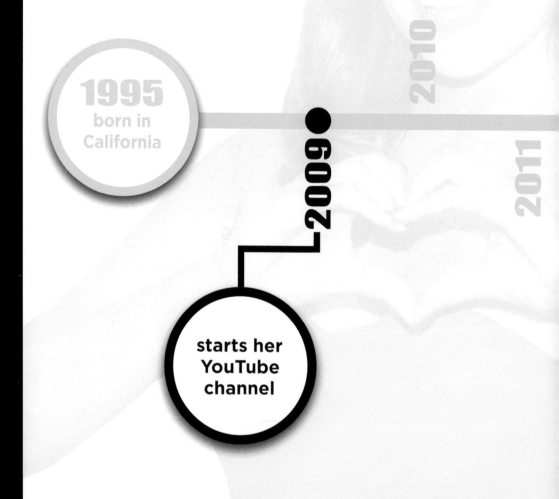

2010

1995
born in
California

2009

2011

starts her
YouTube
channel

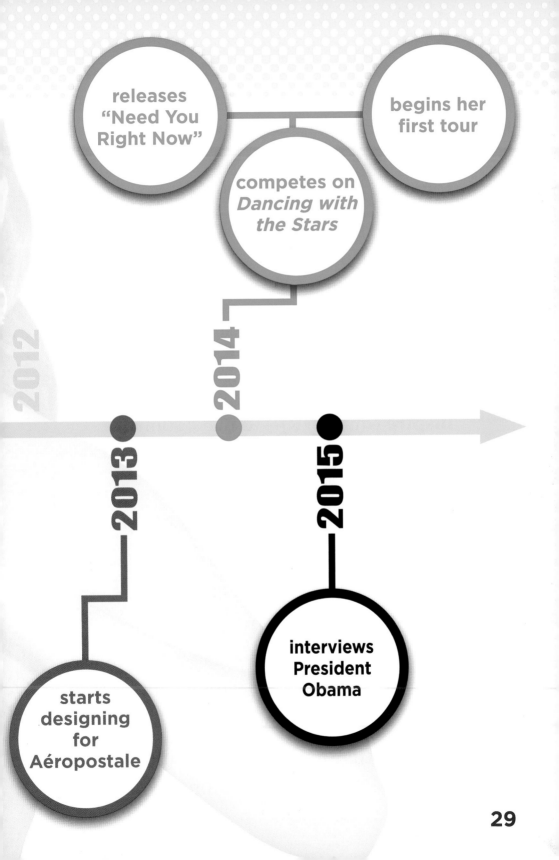

releases "Need You Right Now"

begins her first tour

competes on *Dancing with the Stars*

2012

2014

2013

2015

starts designing for Aéropostale

interviews President Obama

29

cyberbully (SI-bur-bul-ee)—to bully someone online

haul video (HAHL VID-ee-oh)—an online video that shows items that were recently bought

homeschool (HOM-skool)—to teach children at home instead of sending them to school

inspire (in-SPIHR)—to make someone want to do something

interview (IN-tur-vew)—a conversation in which someone asks questions of a person

role model (ROHL MAHD-uhl)—a person whose actions set a good example

UNICEF—stands for United Nations Children's Fund; it's an organization that works to improve the health of children and mothers worldwide.

upload (UP-lohd)—to move a file from a computer or device to a computer network

BOOKS

Klein, Emily. *From Me to YouTube: The Unofficial Guide to Bethany Mota.* New York: Scholastic, 2015.

Minton, Eric. *Cyberbullies. Stay Safe Online.* New York: PowerKids Press, 2014.

Morreale, Marie. *Bethany Mota. Real Bios.* New York: Children's Press, 2016.

WEBSITES

Bethany Mota
www.youtube.com/user/macbarbie07

It's My Life . Friends . Bullies
pbskids.org/itsmylife/friends/bullies/

Stop Bullying.gov
www.stopbullying.gov/kids

INDEX